THE LITTLE BOOK OF

WHISKY

TIPS

Andrew Langley

THE LITTLE BOOK OF

WHISKY

TIPS

Andrew Langley

A.

'Always carry a large flagon of whisky
in case of snakebite, and furthermore
always carry a small snake.'

W.C. Fields

1.

To get the fullest aroma and flavour of a whisky, **drink it from a tulip-shaped 'snifter' glass.** Any whisky will benefit from this sort of respectful attention. As with wines, the narrow top of the glass will concentrate the aroma wonderfully. It will also encourage you to sniff and sip, rather than simply slurp.

To get the fullest aroma and flavour, drink from a tulip-shaped 'snifter' glass.

2. Drink whisky any way you like. There are a thousand different approaches to whisky drinking – with or without ice, water and a vast range of mixers – and none of them is definitively the right one. All the same, **take the time occasionally to savour the drink in its simplest state** – neat or with a little water.

Take the time occasionally to savour the drink in its simplest state.

3. **For cocktails and other mixes, use** one of the **lighter whiskies.** A Canadian, a light Bourbon or a British blend with plenty of grain are best. Heavy malts tend to dominate the taste with their idiosyncratic – though magnificent – qualities.

For cocktails and other mixes, use lighter whiskies.

4. **Serve a good quality single malt at room temperature.** You can even warm the glass with your hands (a good reason for using a stemmed glass). This will gently release the volatile oils and other aromas. If the liquid is too cold, you will miss them.

"Serve a good quality single malt at room temperature."

5. **When flaming a dish in whisky, always heat the spirit** well through **first.** Do this in a tiny saucepan or on a spoon (though very carefully if it's over a naked flame), then pour over and apply a match. Tepid whisky won't light. It will simply soak into the food and make it soggy.

When flaming a dish in whisky, always heat the spirit first.

6.

A highball is the simplest and most famous of all whisky cocktails. Simply a measure of whisky (Bourbon, Irish or blended Scotch) over ice in a tall glass, topped with soda water, it can be decorated with a twist of lemon peel. With rye whisky, use ginger ale instead of soda.

A highball is the simplest
and most famous of all
whisky cocktails.

7. **Coming down with a cold? Try** the classic Scots remedy – **a hot whisky toddy.** Put a measure of whisky, plus the juice of half a lemon, in a glass. Top up with very hot water and stir in a large teaspoonful of honey. Drink as swiftly as possible.

Coming down with a cold? Try a hot whisky toddy.

8. **High-quality Scotch whisky deserves high-quality water.** Tap water will do, as long as you let it stand for a while so that the chlorine can vapourize. However, a still spring water is free of added chemicals which might affect the taste (as is distilled water). Best of all, use burn water gathered near the distillery itself.

"High-quality Scotch whisky deserves high-quality water.

9. **Before putting your Seville orange marmalade into its jars, stir in a shot or two of a blended Scotch whisky.** Do this when the marmalade is still warm, otherwise it won't mix in. Resist the temptation to overdo the whisky – the taste comes through surprisingly strongly.

Before putting your Seville orange marmalade into its jars, stir in a shot or two of a blended Scotch whisky.

10.

Whisky cream is a sensational accompaniment for mince pies. Actually, that should read whiskey cream, because Irish whiskey is the best ingredient. Fold a teaspoon of icing sugar and a shot of whiskey into 285ml (½ pint) of whipped cream. Plonk on mince pies straight from the oven.

Whisky cream is a sensational accompaniment for mince pies.

11.

Should one add water to a good whisky? Some drinkers like it neat, claiming that the delicate purities of aroma and flavour should not be diluted. However, a small amount of water (never more than equal to the liquor) will set off simple chemical reactions which release subtler aspects of both bouquet and taste.

Should one add water to a good whisky?

12.

Great Whisky Combinations No.1: Whisky and prawns. Mix a shot of malt whisky with the same amount of ginger wine, plus a tablespoon of runny honey and some chopped fresh ginger. Use this to marinate 2 diced avocado pears and 225g (8oz) of peeled prawns for 30 minutes. Serve on lettuce with lemon slices.

**Great Whisky Combinations
No.1: Whisky and prawns.**

13.

Atholl brose is an ancient and celebrated Scotch whisky drink. Mix 4 tablepoons of oatmeal with cold water until it becomes a paste. After 30 minutes, strain off the liquid. Mix 3 tablespoons of honey with 600ml (1 pint) of this oatmeal liquid, put into a wine bottle and fill up with malt whisky. Shake well and serve.

Atholl brose is an ancient and celebrated Scotch whisky drink.

14.

When you first pour a good whisky, take time to study its appearance. Swirl the liquid to coat the sides of the glass, and examine the colour and clarity against the light. **The shade of the whisky gives pleasure in itself, but also may provide clues about what vessel it has been aged ('matured') in.**

The shade of the whisky gives pleasure in itself, but also may provide clues about what vessel it has been aged ('matured') in.

15.

At Hogmanay, it is permissible to **douse your haggis with a drop of whisky** from your glass. Purists may shudder, but the the tang of the malt combines perfectly with the pepperiness of the haggis. The better the Scotch, the better the taste.

"At Hogmanay, douse your
haggis with a drop of whisky.

16.

Sazerac is a sensational – if eccentric – **whiskey cocktail from New Orleans.** Stir together a teaspoon of sugar, a dash of Angostura bitters and a shot of rye whiskey. Strain into a glass and add a slug of Pernod or another pastis. Serve with a slice of lemon.

Sazerac is a sensational whiskey cocktail from New Orleans.

17.

Spend some minutes smelling your single malt. 'Nose' plays a big part in the enjoyment of whisky. Put your nose into the top of the glass and sniff, gently at first. Try to identify the different aromas (flowers? seaweed? smoke? pine? honey? salt?). **Swill the whisky and sniff again – you'll get something different this time.**

Swill the whisky and sniff again
– you'll get something different
this time.

18.

If you make your own Christmas puddings, be sure to add some whisky to the mix. **Put in one good shot for every Christmas pudding, but don't be tempted to overdo it.** Too much liquid will stop the pud from cooking properly. The mixture should just drop from the spoon.

Put in one good shot for every Christmas pudding, but don't be tempted to overdo it.

19.

Great Whisky Combinations No.2: Scotch whisky and Scottish Salmon.
Poach 6 salmon steaks. Whisk 3 egg yolks and the juice of a lemon, heating until it thickens in a bowl over boiling water. Stir in 110g (4oz) of butter bit by bit. Remove from the heat and add a shot of whisky and an equal amount of poaching stock. Pour over the steaks and serve.

Great Whisky Combinations No.2: Scotch whisky and Scottish Salmon.

20.

On a cold winter's night, **warm yourself with a hot whisky punch.** Stick 4 cloves into a wedge of lemon. Pop it into a heatproof glass with a big teaspoon of sugar and a shot of whisky (blended Scotch or Irish). The conventional finish is to top up with hot water, however an intriguing alternative is a weak (milkless) Indian tea.

Warm yourself with a hot whisky punch.

21.

Great Whisky Combinations No.3: Whisky and Oranges. Gently heat the juice of one orange with 12 tablespooons of brown sugar, a measure of whisky and an equal amount of water. When mixed, add 3 peeled and thinly sliced oranges and cook for 2–3 minutes. Chill and serve with cream.

Great Whisky Combinations No.3: Whisky and Oranges.

22. Taste is, of course, at the heart of the whisky magic. **Take a sip and roll it round on your tongue.** The spirit will simply evaporate in the mouth, but you should get the 'feel' of the whisky – an infinitely varied combination of sweet and dry, cream and pepper, smoke and honey. Dream up your own description.

Take a sip and roll it round on your tongue.

23.

Here's a variation on the much-loved Irish coffee phenomenon, made in heaven to be poured on ice cream. Heat a syrup of 75ml (3fl oz) of water and 225g (8oz) of sugar gently until it caramelises. Then stir in 225ml (8fl oz) of fresh-made coffee and let cool. Finally, add a measure of good Irish whiskey (no cream!).

"Here's a variation on the much-loved Irish coffee phenomenon..."

24.

If you build up a whisky collection, take the trouble to store your bottles safely. Store bottles away from direct sunlight (which can affect the colour of the spirit and bleach the label) and in a cool, dry and stable place. **Unlike wine, whisky bottles can be kept upright:** a little alcohol will vaporize and keep the cork moist.

Unlike wine, whisky bottles can be kept upright.

25.

Whisky often makes an intriguing alternative to cognac or calvados in meat dishes. Brown two veal escalopes and a cubed apple in butter, then flambe with a shot of warmed whisky until the flames die down. Stir in 150ml (¼ pint) of single cream and cook gently for a couple of minutes. Serve with apples and sauce on top.

Whisky often makes an intriguing alternative to cognac or calvados in meat dishes.

26.

After sipping your whisky and feeling it in the mouth, **wait for the finish.** This consists of the flavours which arrive after the liquid itself has gone. These may include vanilla, wood and even salt, and may be long and warming or short and dry. The longer the finish, the better (and older) the whisky.

After sipping your whisky, wait for the finish.

27. Japanese whisky can be an astoundingly good – if expensive – accompaniment for Japanese food. This is especially true of sushi. **The malty flavours of the whisky marry well with the sweetness of soy sauce or miso,** while its salty feel is echoed by the seafood and seaweed dishes.

The malty flavours of the whisky marry well with the sweetness of soy sauce or miso.

28.

The Whiskey Collins cocktail is named after its inventor, the celebrated US bartender Tom Collins. In a shaker, blend some ice, a shot of Bourbon, the juice from 2 lemons and a teaspoon of powdered sugar. Strain into a glass. Add orange and lemon slices and top with a cherry. Straw advisable.

The Whiskey Collins cocktail is named after its inventor.

29.

How long does a whisky last? The short answer is – indefinitely, as long as it is sealed in an unopened bottle. Whisky is matured in oak casks, which allow it to breathe and develop. Once it is bottled, the breathing stops and the liquor goes into suspended animation. 'Laid down' bottles will not improve with age.

"How long does a whisky last?"

30.

**Great Whisky Combinations
No.4: Whisky and Chocolate.**
Put 6 crushed chocolate digestive
biscuits in a dish. Whip up 600ml
(1 pint) of sugared cream and a shot
of whisky, then fold in 2 whipped
egg whites. Lay the mixture over
the crushed biscuits, and top with
grated chocolate and toasted flaked
almonds.

"Great Whisky Combinations
No.4: Whisky and Chocolate."

31.

Always read the label on the bottle.
This can tell you a lot. For instance,
something called Scottish Whiskey
(rather than Scotch Whisky) will
probably be anything but. The label
should also define whether it is
'Blended' (a mix of malt and grain
whiskies), 'Malt Whisky' (a mix of
malts) or 'Single Malt' (not mixed in
any way).

"Always read the label on the bottle.

32.

A Rusty Nail brings together two great Scottish institutions. Pour a shot of blended Scotch over ice in a tumbler. Then gently add a measure of Drambuie, pouring it over the back of a teaspoon so thatit floats on top of the whisky.

A Rusty Nail brings together two great Scottish institutions.

33.

Irish whiskey and seafood are made for each other. Soften 6 sliced leeks in oil for 10 minutes. Remove, add more oil and sear two dozen scallops for 2 minutes a side. Remove these and degrease the pan with a shot of good Irish whiskey. Stir in 3 tablespoons of cream and pour over the leeks and scallops.

"Irish whiskey and seafood are made for each other.

34. **Here's another surprising marriage of whisky and orange.** Place 4 slices each of peeled orange, peeled lemon and fresh pineapple in a blender. Whizz briefly then add a large measure of blended Scotch or bourbon and a generous dash of Orange Curacao and whizz again. Pour over ice.

"Here's another surprising marriage of whisky and orange..."

35.

For the legendary Manhattan cocktail, a sweet vermouth is mixed with double the quantity of rye or bourbon whiskey. This is stirred with ice, strained into a glass and topped with a cherry. **For a dry Manhattan –** less well-known – **substitute dry for sweet vermouth, and an olive for the cherry.**

For a dry Manhattan, substitute dry for sweet vermouth, and an olive for the cherry.

36.

Single malt whiskies usually have their age stated on the label (something like 'Aged 12 Years'). This indicates the time spent maturing in cask before bottling. Some bottles – confusingly – instead declare the distillation date and the bottling date. The age will be the difference between the two.

Single malt whiskies usually have their age stated on the label.

37. **Does your whisky go hazy when you add water or ice?** Rejoice. You are drinking one of the few whiskies (such as the great Springbank) to have escaped chill filtration. This cosmetic process removes compounds which cause hazing. Some believe it also removes some of the whisky's special flavour and feel.

"Does your whisky go hazy when you add water or ice?"

38.

Jazz up pork or gammon steaks with an Irish whiskey sauce. Fry 4 steaks in butter for 8 minutes a side. Remove and fry a chopped onion. Stir in 30g (1oz) of flour – slowly – and then 150ml (¼ pint) of stock and a tablespoon of sugar. Finally bung in a measure of Irish whiskey, heat and pour over the steaks.

"Jazz up pork or gammon steaks with an Irish whiskey sauce.

39. When it first comes from the still, **whisky is naturally colourless.** The colour of the bottled stuff usually comes from two sources. One is the wood in which the spirit is aged (new oak for bourbon, for example, or old sherry casks for some Scotches). The other is – unromantically – sugar caramel.

"Whisky is naturally colourless.

40.

Old Fashioned is the name, but this whiskey cocktail has been in fashion for over a century. Put a lump of sugar in a short, squat glass and soak with a drop or two of Angostura bitters. Squash the sugar with a spoon and stir in a shot of rye or bourbon. Add ice and a twist of lemon peel.

"Old Fashioned is the name, but this whiskey cocktail has been in fashion for over a century."

41.

How long does a bottle of whisky last once opened? It depends on how much is left. When you open a bottle, you let in air. This immediately starts to react with the whisky, releasing volatile elements such as the alcohol and aromas. A near-empty bottle contains a lot of air, and will lose its 'edge' very swiftly.

How long does a bottle of whisky last once opened?

42.

Cauliflower cheese is transformed by a touch of whisky. Blanch the florets for 5 minutes, drain and put in an ovenproof dish. Heat 300ml (½ pint) of double cream, stirring in grated Cheddar cheese. Away from the heat, add a double shot of Scotch and a tablespoon of fine oatmeal. Pour over the cauliflower and bake for 45 minutes.

Cauliflower cheese is transformed by a touch of whisky.

43. **Great Whisky Combinations No.5: Whisky and Figs.** Gently poach some dried figs in water. Then drain and steep them in Irish whiskey for at least 24 hours. This heavenly marriage of tastes was invented by a descendant of Napoleon in the mid-nineteenth century.

Great Whisky Combinations No.5: Whisky and Figs.

44.

A mint julep is the classic beverage for spectators of the Kentucky Derby. Boil up a syrup of equal parts sugar and water. Cool and refrigerate overnight with a handful of fresh mint. Next day, put crushed ice in a julep cup and add a tablespoon of the mint syrup and a slug of Kentucky whisky. Stir and garnish with a sprig of mint.

A mint julep is the classic beverage for spectators of the Kentucky Derby.

45.

Scottish island malts such as a Lagavulin or an Ardbeg **go particularly well with blue cheese.** The smokiness of the peat and the iodine taste of the sea are a feisty match for the pungency of a Gorgonzola or a Roquefort. Better still, try a fine Scottish-produced cheese such as Lanarkshire Blue or Dunsyre Blue.

Scottish island malts go particularly well with blue cheese.

46.

Whisky matures more quickly in hot climates. Therefore spirit from warm regions such as the southern USA, India, Spain, Tennessee and Turkey will reach a drinkable age when comparatively young. **Whiskies from colder places, such as New Zealand, Canada and of course Scotland, will mature when rather older.**

Whiskies from colder places, such as New Zealand, Canada and of course Scotland, will mature when rather older.

47.

A whisky eggnog is a great pick-me-up (known by Scots as 'Auld man's Milk'). Put ice, 230ml (8fl oz) of milk, a double shot of blended Scotch, a raw egg and a teaspoon of sugar into a shaker. Shake energetically and pour into a glass. Grate some nutmeg on top and drink.

A whisky eggnog is a great pick-me-up.

48.

When planning your Christmas cake, remember to start the day before you bake. This gives you time to **measure out the dried fruit and soak it overnight in whisky.** This will plump it up and make the end result much moister – and tastier.

When planning your Christmas
cake, measure out the dried
fruit and soak it overnight
in whisky.

49.

The Robbie Burns cocktail is a bizarre tribute to Scotland's greatest poet but he'd have loved it. Fill a cocktail shaker with ice, a shot of sweet vermouth, a shot of blended Scotch and a shot of Benedictine. Shake and strain into a glass. Serve with a twist of lemon peel.

The Robbie Burns cocktail is
a bizarre tribute to Scotland's
greatest poet.

50. **Most of the whisky you buy already has water in it.** The spirit in the cask contains 50–60 per cent of alcohol by volume (this is the 'cask strength'). The majority of whiskies are then cut (diluted) with distilled water down to about 40–46 per cent by volume. Cask strength whisky is available in special bottlings.

"Most of the whisky you buy
already has water in it."

Andrew Langley

Andrew Langley is **a knowledgeable food and drink writer.** Among his formative influences he lists a season picking grapes in Bordeaux, several years of raising sheep and chickens in Wiltshire and two decades drinking his grandmother's tea. He has written books on a number of Scottish and Irish whisky distilleries and is the editor of the highly regarded anthology of the writings of the legendary Victorian chef Alexis Soyer.

"A knowledgeable food
and drink writer."

**Little Books of Tips from
Absolute Press**

Aga	Gardening
Allotment	Gin
Avocado	Golf
Beer	Herbs
Cake Decorating	Spice
Cheese	Tea
Coffee	Whisky
Fishing	Wine

If you enjoyed this book, try...

THE LITTLE BOOK OF

WINE

TIPS

Store your wine somewhere cool and very slightly humid.

Keep your wine glasses stored the right way up.

Absolute Press

An imprint of Bloomsbury Publishing Plc

50 Bedford Square	1385 Broadway
London	New York
WC1B 3DP	NY 10018
UK	USA

www.bloomsbury.com

ABSOLUTE PRESS and the A. logo are trademarks of Bloomsbury Publishing Plc

First published in 2007
This edition printed 2017

© Andrew Langley, 2007
Cover image: TS Photography / Getty Images

Andrew langley has asserted his right under the Copyright, Designs and Patents Act, 1988, to be identified as Author of this work.

A catalogue record for this book is available from the British Library.
Library of Congress Cataloguing-in-Publication data has been applied for.
ISBN 13: 9781472954534

Printed and bound in Spain by Tallers Grafics Soler